Heart and Soul
Book of Lyrics

By T.L. Raasch

Table of Contents

1. Rejection to Acception

(3 minutes 26 Seconds)
By T.L. Raasch

NOTE: I went to a writing seminar once. It seemed to me that most writer agents are women. This is just an observation not a political statement. Also, I was warned at this seminar that a male author's work doesn't sell nearly as well has well as female's work. I know they were just being straight with all us newbies, telling us this, but this little fact is why my books and now my CD show T.L. Raasch as the author.

Any way, this song is a story about a brand new author trying to get an agent to represent his work to publishers and or bookstores. Like fishing, he sends out line after line to agent after agent, and finally one bites and the process begins. This is actually where this song begins.

The agent tells her (or his) new client, "You need to react to my change suggestions immediately, for time is money." At this point in the process, in order to keep her on the hook and interested, the author will agree to most anything.

When the agent's suggestions begin to come in the author initially agrees to make some enhancements, even when the changes seem to change the meaning slightly. As more and more changes are suggested he realizes this is no longer his work, or his intention so the agent becomes an antagonist and eventually his enemy.

In the end, an author like myself just self publishes his work on his own. Of course he has no one to promote his work, so he sells nothing. He reverts to distributing his work to friends and acquaintances for free.

I suppose you'll ask, "Why would he do such a thing?" Well, his love is the writing and his readership is simply the dessert. And like anyone else, he simply loves dessert.

Final NOTE: About the title, the word, "Acception" is not really a word (at least I don't think it is) but it is meant to be a perfect antonym to the word "Rejection".

<u>The Lyrics</u>

I've got my finger on your pulse.
I'm ready to sing your tune
Or dance the waltz.
(Yes, I'll sing and dance for you.)

You're waiting there in the judge's chamber
You've got your chopping block and saber.
(I fear your saber the most.)

Finally, the bell tolls upon my masterpiece.
(I lay my masterpiece at your feet.)
I think it's done, but you return it.
You said, "The clever twisting spots need to
be re-worded."
(I don't think you get it, but I'll rewrite it
anyway.)

I search through my pockets for the proper
change
It needs to be unique and appropriately
strange.
(I really don't like these changes.)

I look upon my shelf for a new word,
or a shifted letter.

I put on old shoes to swerve the plot,
to make it swift and better.
(But these changes don't make it
more swift or more clever.)

After due consideration,
I realize it's not the scene or characters.
Perhaps just a costume switch.
But is it hers, or his, or is it both, or which?

(Why in the name of literature are we
listening to this crazy bitch?)

We second-guess ourselves to a fault,
(But it's not our fault.)
It seems all our best-phrased words are
stranded in their vault.
Could it be that "To be or not to be?"
wouldn't be their question?
And not because, or why, but merely their
suggestion.

Imagine this submission:
"Declaration of Independence" sincerely TJ
And the subsequent rejection,
"Please word it another way."

2. Idiot Me
(4 minutes 11 Seconds)
By T.L. Raasch
(A reflection of Bob Dylan's Idiot Wind)

I love the Bob Dylan song called "Idiot Wind". Here I re-wrote the first 2 stanza's keeping many of the words, but shuffling them to create a brand new meaning and a brand new tone. Then added some musical chords and made it my own.

<u>Dylan's Lyrics for Idiot Wind</u>

Someone's got it in for me
They're planting stories in the press
Whoever it is I wish they'd cut it out quick
But when they will I can only guess
They say I shot a man named Gray
And took his wife to Italy
She inherited a million bucks
And when she died it came to me
I can't help it if I'm lucky

People see me all the time
And they just can't remember how to act
Their minds are filled with big ideas
Images and distorted facts.

Even you, yesterday
You had to ask me where it was at
I couldn't believe after all these years
You didn't know me better than that
Sweet lady

The idiot wind blowing every time
you move your mouth
Blowing down the back roads headin' south
The idiot wind blowing every time
you move your teeth.
You're an idiot, babe it's a wonder that
you still know how to breathe.

I ran into the fortune-teller
Who said, "Beware of lightning that might
strike."
I haven't known peace and quiet for so long I
can't remember what it's like.
There's a lone soldier on the cross, smoke
pourin' out of a boxcar door.
You didn't know it, you didn't think
it could be done.
In the final end he won the wars after losin'
every battle.

I woke up on the roadside
daydreamin' 'bout the way thing

sometimes are.
Visions of your chestnut mare shoot through
my head and are makin' me see stars.
You hurt the ones that I love best and cover
up the truth with lies.
One day you'll be in the ditch, flies buzzin'
around your eyes, blood on your saddle

The idiot wind blowing through
the flowers on your tomb.
Blowing through the curtains in your room
The idiot wind blowing every time
you move your teeth.
You're an idiot, babe, it's a wonder that
You still know how to breathe.

<u>My Lyrics to "Idiot Me"</u>

Someone was coming here for me.
She was an unexpected guest.
I didn't know her very well,
Couldn't say if I was cursed or blessed.
Her reason was a shade of grey,
Why she came she didn't say.
When someone said, "She's worth a million
bucks" I had to say, "Oh really?"
Was I suddenly lucky?

I thought about her all the time.
I kept imaging our wedding bells.
My mind was filled with big ideas,
images of instant wealth.
As recent as yesterday
I had detailed plans all worked out.
I couldn't see no reason
For even a shadow of a doubt.
It was insanity!
Ah the idiot me, windblown fool's gold
in my eyes.
Reality was twisted in with lies.
The idiot me, my mind cluttered in confusion
I was an idiot all right, a victim
of such delusion.

I invited her to see a fortune-teller.
She said "Beware of fools like me."
I haven't seen her even once since.
Why she left is no mystery.
She left in such a hurry
I saw smoke pouring from her exhaust.
Now I'm all alone again,
But the memory of her isn't lost
She's simply gone.

Now all I do is dream
About the way things were with her.
I'm all choked up inside,
My eyes are wet and my vision's blurred.
I lost the one I love best,
Foiled by that soothsayer spy.
Yes I blame it on that fortune-bitch,
For making me so traumatized.
Blame where it belongs.

The idiot me, blowing up a brand new
hot-air balloon
Circling the sky in search of Brigadoon
The idiot me, expected something
just like Camelot
I was an idiot all right, 'cause empty dreams
are all I got.

3. The Ol' Face Dilemma

(3 minutes 1 Second)
By T.L. Raasch

If there was such a thing, I would declare this next piece my greatest hit. When introducing a new reader to my work, I generally present this one first. It's relatable and understandable.

<u>The Lyrics</u>

I'm frustrated!
I have this amazin' face
Yet I feel I must trade it.
You see, when I look in the mirror,
The same ol' image appears.
I close my eyes, it disappears,
But I'll open them again
'n hope against hope
That yesterday's image'll appear.
Nope. Nothing's replaced.

Jest the same ol' dope
with a clown's face 'n a frown in place.
I swear, I'll drowned in waste
If I don't get to the bottom of this,
post haste.

I'm bound 'n determine to chase down jest
what happened to this face.
Jest who in God's name would
arrange a change like this?
It seems kinda strange that anyone would
approve an exchange like this.
Jest who's to blame, 'n what's his name?
I kinda wanna inflict
The same kinda mischief
On him 'n his kin if in fact, he is a 'him',
'n even if he's a 'her' it's a sin!

Jest who made me look like
the survivin' twin with a wrinkled chin 'n
hair all grey-speckled 'n thinned.
I swear, I never did do nothing to him.

Jest who was it that took my good looks
'n buried them away in one of those
picture books.
Who's the crook who left me sittin' here,
With chin 'n hands, tryin' to understand
Why I appear as I appear. It's just weird!

Clearly all my youthfulness has left me
It's erased and disappeared.
And it's left me a bit bitter, but really

that ol' face ain't a bit better
Jest different than the replacement face
that's starin' me in the eye
with all God's wisdom planted in place.
As days go bye,
I realize it ain't no mistake
'n it's jest a disgrace to want
this amazin' replacement face erased.

4. Shiver Me Timbers

(3 minutes 4 Second)
By Tom Waits

This is a Tom Waits cover about a young man leaving the nest. He believes his calling is to the sea. It's not an easy decision, as he believes he must sacrifice his family and friends to really get the true romantic experience.

In the end, the living fantasy is too alluring to resist, so he leaves without really saying good-bye. He seemingly doesn't want to be followed or dissuaded.

<u>The Lyrics</u>

Well I'm leavin' my family,
Leavin' my friends.
My body's at home,
But my heart's in the wind
Where the clouds are like headlines,
On a new front page sky
My tears are salt water
The moon's full and high.

And I know my comrades
Are gonna be proud of me
And the many before me
Who've been called by the sea
To be up in the crow's nest
Singin' my say
Oh, shiver me timbers,
I'm a-sailin' away

The fog's liftin' ,the sand's shiftin',
I'm driftin' on out,
and ol' Captain Ahab
Ain't got nothin' on me.
So come on and swallow me,
Don't follow me,
I'm traveling alone.
Blue water's my daughter,
I skip like a stone.

Please call my family,
Tell 'em not to cry.
My goodbye is written,
By the moon in the sky
And nobody knows me,
I got no reason to stay,
So shiver me timbers,
I'm sailin' away . . .

5. She's Put A Spell On You

(2 minutes 37 Seconds)
By T.L. Raasch

Simply put, this is a love story. She works in the kitchen of her quiet homestead, conjuring up a magical brew. It's design is specifically directed at an unsuspecting you.

Her potion, its taste and aroma are too powerful for you to resist, and so you fall victim to it's controlling spell and you love every minute. Meanwhile, everyone else thinks you are a lovesick fool for it affects only you.

The Lyrics

She's put a spell on you.
She's compelled to overwhelm you.
She stirs her magical brew.
The aroma is alluring to you.

The spell begins and ends on Halloween.
'n remains all the days in between.
Her hypnotic words controlling you.
Every word she speaks seems like a rule.

"Jump! Dance!" she laughs at you.
To you she seems romantically cool.
Only you are affected by this wicked stew.
No one else has a clue.

They ridicule the things you do.
It really doesn't matter
For she's the one you love,
And she loves you.

6. A Ballad of Sweet Old Insecurity

(7 minutes 52 Seconds)
By T.L. Raasch

This is meant to be duet, sung by a husband and wife. There's no background music for this song, just raw emotion.

Lying in bed, she is keeping him awake as she ponders and yearns for something; he is unaware of what? When she says she just needs to feel more loved he reacts in a lighthearted manner at first. This reaction just brings her more urgency and more uneasiness from her.

Soon he realizes the seriousness so he verbally works to relieve her doubts. After a fashion, he realizes she just wants to hear a simple, "I love you." She confesses it's not for her, but rather it's for her sweet insecurity.

In a twist at the end, he finds he's falling victim to the same sort of insecurity.

The Lyrics

She's lyin' there, just starin' at the ceiling
If something's troubling her, she's not
revealing it to me
Then she turns and whispers . . .

I've got this question for ya Mister
But I get the feeling you won't tell me the
truth.

Then why on earth should I answer?
If not believing me is what you choose.
I'm only gonna lose,

But I wanna know right now, "Do you love
me?"

The question you pose, there's only one
answer, "No!"

Oh no! How could you say such a thing?
When you know I'm feeling so low.

Well I wanted you to be right, so we could
turn out the light
And say good night.

It ain't right you know, when you make light
of me
I only wanted you to enlighten me.

Oh alright, ask the question again without
your preferences
And I'll try to make some sense of this.

You need to understand this
This won't be the last time I asked this. "Do
you love me?"

I close my eyes to contemplate (oh no)
I'm Just searching for the way to express it
best.

There should be no need to contemplate.
I'm not seeking any of your cleverness.

Please look in my eyes
Can't you just see what you mean to me?

She closes her eyes and shakes her head
No I can't, I really can't see what you see in
me.

I grab her arm and shake it, Honey I know
you can't see it

But surely you should feel it and know it's
true.

She smiles but there's a tear in her eye
I only feel uneasiness, my confidence is
shaking
And now I wonder if you're only faking.

You need to stop right there
And try to recall all the good times we've
shared.
Yes we've stumbled through some troubles
But we've been together seems like forever
And I can't imagine without you, even for
never.
I'm just not that clever.
Why can't you see you're my baby?
And don't you know you're my inner soul,
you're my angel.
No, I don't have an angle.
I've just written you these words, sang you
my song
Been your children's father,
Been your life long lover, I've never dreamed
of another
And I've never left you standing, never left
you sad.

Why can't you see, what all these
circumstances mean?

You need to understand, though your
evidence is substantial
It seems to me circumstantial.
That's why I need to hear it every day,
That you love me.
All this is really not for me,
It's for sweet insecurity.
She's not logical.
She's just an emotional hunger.
And I guess I'm getting older,
'cause I can't control her any longer.

It's all so clear, it's not about her
It's about this damn insecurity.
I guess I'm getting older too
I just felt the tap on my shoulder
And it's like I told her
I can't see it,
But I sure can feel it
And know it's true.
And now it's me with sweet insecurity
And my mind is reeling.
I'm lying here just looking at the ceiling
Wondering when she will be revealing,
What it is, she needs from me.

7. Wedding Song

(3 minutes 39 Seconds)
Written by Bob Dylan

This is a fitting follow-up tune, written by Bob Dylan. He is simply professing his love for his wife. I find the lyrics to be very powerful, but just as circumstantial.

<u>Dylan's Lyrics</u>

I love you more than ever,
more than time and more than love
I love you more than money
And more than the stars above
Love you more than madness,
More than dreams upon the sea
Love you more than life itself,
You mean that much to me.

Ever since you walked right in,
The circle's been complete
I've said goodbye to haunted rooms
And faces in the street
From the courtyard of the jester
Which is hidden from the sun
I love you more than ever

And I haven't yet begun.

You breathed on me
And made my life a richer one to live
When I was deep in poverty
You taught me how to give
Dried the tears up from my dreams
And pulled me from the hole
Quenched my thirst and
Satisfied the burning in my soul.

The tune that is yours and
Mine to play upon the earth
We'll play it out the best we know,
Whatever it is worth
What's lost is lost,
We can't regain what went down in the flood
But happiness to me is you
And I love you more than blood.

It's never been my duty
To remake the world at large
Nor is it my intention
To sound a battle charge
'Cause I love you more than all of that
With a love that doesn't bend
And if there is eternity

I'll love you there again.

Oh, can't you see that
You were born to stand by my side
And I was born to be with you,
You were born to be my bride
You're the other half of what I am,
You're the missing piece
And I love you more than ever
With that love that doesn't cease.

You turn the tide on me each day
And teach my eyes to see
Just bein' next to you
Is a natural thing for me
And I could never let you go,
No matter what goes on
'Cause I love you more than ever
Now that the past is gone.

8. Flavor and Color

(2 minutes 54 Seconds)
by T.L. Raasch

This is just a visual "fantasy" piece. Close your eyes and imagine you're dreaming a senseless dream.

Don't look for any kind of underlying meaning. As the author, I'm not sure there is one.

Of course I'm more than willing to listen to your ideas, if you think you've discovered something.

<u>The Lyrics</u>

There's a paradise of flavor and color
Invite your sisters and your brother
And I shouldn't have to tell you
Invite your father and your mother too.

Don't forget your umbrella
For its raining corn curls
The ground is covered with jellybean pearls
And please don't step upon
The little melting chocolate girls.

Honey leaves dripping from the trees
It's the cakes icing, if you please
With all the powdered sugar,
Be careful not to sneeze

Put a rope 'round lemon mountain
And squeeze the juice to a jell-o fountain
Then lick the sticky fingers
On which you're a-countin on.

Coconuts flakes snow down from the sky
Where only cherry flavored bluebirds fly
And Toucans can too, if they try.

The oranges are orange and marmalade
With grapes growing wild
In the purple shade
Using just imagination,
The fantasy's displayed.

9. Carrie Mae Dephardt and Stalker McGee

(6 minutes 12 Seconds)
By T.L. Raasch

This powerful piece asks, "What's worse?"

You being very much in love with someone who has no plans for you?
or
You having someone totally smitten with you, and she (or he) is constantly trying to be with you and to gain your affection. In this case, you aren't the least bit interested, and as time wears on, so does your patience.

A little author insight, the title could read something like this

"Carrie may depart and someone is stalking me!"

The Lyrics

What is it about Carrie Mae Dephardt? I know she comes from the darker side just across the railroad tracks, and while others

are busy looking down at her, I'm simply
infatuated by her mystic, sorcerous charms.

Those black shiny boots with the silver
spurs move in time with the music inside
her head 'n using a pied-piper technique
somehow her hips 'n free-flowing hair keep
independently synchronized.

Her snowflake quips are light and innocent
when left to land and merely melt, but if
they drift together they concoct a compelling
potion too powerful for ordinary resistance.

One after one, those words roll off her lips 'n
snowball down toward me exclusively. They
are magnificent; a magnetic attraction to
which I'm the victim.

There was a time we laid together; her
tongue licked her lips and then she touched
mine. I breathed her breath, caging the very
essence of her soul within me.

Day after day I prayed she'd seek my
shoulder to cry upon, to carry her burden,
but when the night finally fell the beautiful
beast up and left me . . . bleeding.

She never was equipped to take on prisoners, so she cracked her whip toward the exit 'n the whirling winds brought shivers, I quivered as she vanished in a whisper.

Beset, her fading, echoing void renders me empty, I surrender no more significant than a yawn at sunset; still I miss her.

I still hear the howling, envision her silhouette. The haunting image of a fire red mustang chained to the stake through my heart. Her twisting emotions of leather remain wind-blown scattered to all the corners of my consciousness.

Carrie Mae Dephardt is my phantom pain; there is no cure. The chokehold she has on me is irrational, yet I'm resigned to her emotional dominance. I reckon its desperation, my reigns of hope tied directly to her unlikely acceptance.

*** *** ***

Those psychological shackles are no more or less restricting than the ones applied by my very own sycophant; let's call her Stalker McGee. It was some time ago now that the curse began her attraction to me, that is.

She approached as a stray little kitten, our paths crossed, she brushed my leg 'n purred just below my awareness. She flew in undetected past my superficial radar gun.

Her camouflaged plumage was void of any 'n all the elements I find alluring. I was indifferent toward her, but remained polite banking on her bolting due to her expected fleeting level of addiction.

Instead she lingered, gradually gaining my confidence with a light-hearted casual banter. Too soon it became mundane lacking in any kind of substance that would sustain my interest.

She hovers over me. A black umbrella with a hole in it. The steady drip, drip, drip of her presence forms beads of liquid rollin' down my nose into my space, attacking my nerves. Everywhere I turn I feel her burn, my stomach churns.

I caught her tailgating, her bright lights filling my mirror blinding my view to anything else. Her persistence grows; a lap dog nipping at my heels 'n wearing out my patience. And grows some more; a guard dog warding off my friends 'n scarring my social reputation.

When McGee finally got her claws in me she wouldn't let go and everywhere I am she lurks. She's a cobra now hanging above my door, peering into my window waiting for the perfect opportunity to wrap her ever-loving arms around my neck.

She's even there waiting when my bus arrives, offering to give me a ride in her crashed up automobile. I swear I never did do something to encourage this behavior.

*** *** ***

You know they say there is no hope if you can't see options. I'm optimistic. I gaze into the crystal ball, looking for another side. I contemplate, sort and categorize all the available options 'n in the end I only see but two homicide or . . . suicide.

Now I ask you, what's worse than that?

10. Friends Don't Let Friends Fall

(2 minutes 49 Seconds)
By T.L. Raasch

This is a good follow-up song to the previous, as this person may have found something worse than the situations defined above.

Here, she (or he) seems to feel she is on the outside looking in with her 3 friends. Maybe she feels like a "black sheep" or something.

Anyway, she is lonely and desperate for a feeling of inclusion. This story ends tragically.

The Lyrics

I'm lonely, in need of a friend.
The 3 of you think you know me,
But in the end I'm nestled up here,
My legs curled up under a truth that's
staring me in the face,
I need space to gather my emotions.
The very notion
That you understand escapes me
For I've search the world end to end
Looking for a friend
Who'd be willing to pull me from the ledge
Yet I'm still on the brink
'n I get the distinct impression
You all are merely guessing how I feel.

The 3 of you have just one heart, one brain,
One state of mind that can't be separated
So if one of you doesn't get it,
None of you gets it, so you can't fix it;
If indeed you really do care, I missed it.
I've got a brand new rope
Wwrapped around my neck
And the chair below me is teetering.
Why can't even one of you
Make the effort to break my fall?

It just breaks my heart
To think you're all so small.

Ah, it's too late to open your heart
To be my friend.
Now I'm simply seeking
Some senseless revenge.
I want you and you and yes even you
To rip open your shirt,
Imagine a target on you.
Displayed in bright red paint.
Want u to know the difference between
indifference and hate.
You ignored me when I needed you most.
I, on the other hand,
Had my gun locked and loaded.
I've since changed my mind,
I'm falling fast, soon to be gone
Don't worry those bullets won't be exploded.
Yes, you'll only have these memories of me
And the knowledge that I'm completely
resting in peace.

11. Which Way Is Up
(3 minutes 5 Seconds)
By T.L. Raasch

And this one is a good follow-up to the follow-up. The question here is, "What makes a person popular?" or "Why are some people in the "cool group", while others are prohibited?"

Adding to the dimension of this song, I pretend to be working in a music studio, arranging the instrumental portions.

It begins, the producer (me) is directing the band for the inclusion of some background instruments; drums, a piano and some strings, but as they do the I order them to pull them out as the mood they've created seems to be too dramatic for what is intended.

The band tries again, this time producing a more restrained and mellow tone, pleasing the producer. The producer then directs the singer to proceed, and he likes what he hears. On the count of four, the new song begins, but as it progresses the band adds back the original drama as they are seemingly moved by the lyrics. I hope this song is as moving for you as the band indicates.

<u>The Lyrics</u>

Oh I don't know why "the ins" are in,
And I don't know why the "the outs" are out.
I don't even know which way is up,
And I sure don't know how to reverse
or turn about.

Well I just want to be me,
Without any apology.
I want to release the "what I was"
And set it free.

I want the "who I am",
To be the "what you grasp",
Not that "what's his name",
The "who I was" from the past.
And I just want you to be pure and true,
Not that "used to be one",

the "one I knew".

Your history is maintained by other
people's point of view.
It's established by the limits
of what they know and knew about you.
With this they try to set your bar,
and make your rules.

If only your history were a mystery,
With no references and was missing
all the clues.
Those people who thought they knew you
Couldn't lock you in or kick you out.
It is indeed your history that allows
them to remove this doubt.

12. The Jungle
(3 minutes 55 Seconds)
By T.L. Raasch

I've never been to a jungle, but here I try to paint with words my image of what it would be like to be in a jungle. I added some background music and in one take the song I was trying to produce came into being.

<u>The Lyrics</u>

The jungle seduces
even the most uncivilized of beasts.
It reduces a lion to its knees
And induces the dark black panther to pant.
A bushmaster slithers
Down a poisonous twisting path
Leading to the echoing caves,
Complete with organic slaves
And volcanic ash covered skeletal remains.

Leaves draped,
Clinging to vines ever so loosely
Dripping wet, falling to an autumn floor
Closing the door on private mysterious eyes.
Smoky mist shadows silhouettes

Hunting and stalking,
Daring to walk inside cool dampness.

Cracked shells of oyster innocence
Swallow the scent of moisture
Streaming down a motionless path
Wishing to touch newborn twigs
Springing up between tulips griping the soil.
The temptress fig entices wasp after wasp
To a passage too narrow, foiling their exit.

The blistering sun politely warms
Storms arousing and
Probing virgin openings
A natural knife breathing in life
So spine tingling precise.
All the species co-mingle 'n socialize,
Drink nectar from forbidden honey
Sweet upon the lips of the lucky ones
Who suck the sticky mellow
Swelling in the loins of untouched foliage.

Dandelions changing their colors
so all can see
Planting seeds in a camouflaged cradle
The tender, the gentle, the ever so fragile.
Blowing winds whisper
And willows weep rainbows

Daises cry beneath the nightingale skies.

And so it goes and then it snows.
Frozen ground around hollows
Ice sickles waiting for another cycle
Mango fruits 'n tangled up spices
Ripening and exciting the dormant,
Hibernating bears, the bare naked trees.
All the individual senses undressed
In the wide-open eyes of the wilderness.

13. In A Nutshell
(12 minutes 41 Seconds)
T.L. Raasch

In keeping with the jungle theme, this song tries to move you through life itself, from beginning to end. It's a "In a Nutshell" capsulation, using a virtual jungle as its vehicle. As various animals and circumstances are introduced, the hope is you'll say, "I know a guy like this" or "Yep, I know exactly what the song is getting at."

<u>The Lyrics</u>

Eight . . . nine . . . ten . . . Month after month it seems so little is happening, and then, "Okay, let's get her started. Remember to breathe . . . focus and breathe".

Everything begins inside the womb. For some, the contractions cause pain, but for the rest of us it's just a container. We are determined to sustain. We take a slow ride on a slow boat looking for a golden bowl to hold all the fruits of our labor. Aided by an easterly sea breeze, we push along in peaceful security and the comforting support of our neighbors.

A sudden unexpected rush of a hurricane wind knocks the very foundation of our journey and there are consequences. The turmoil and flooding have left us stranded on the rocks just outside our comfort zone

But we come to our senses and find we're docked just two or three miles closer to our destiny. The clock says we've arrived unexpectedly early by a minute or two . . . or perhaps it's a day or even a year, but this is a minimal distinction. In shock and in fear we abandon our path only to find a virtual jungle; complete with one thousand middle-aged runaway elephants, escaping from their inevitable extinction. Yes their numbers are dwindling, far faster than expected and we determine the reduction is natural, but far less than acceptable, and I told you for some contractions are painful.

"Stop! Focus and breathe."

Ah, the road from here is filled with winter potholes, covered with fig leaves and lined with temptation apple trees and samples of things that should 'n shouldn't be.

There is an abundance of essentials that just happen to reside just out of the reach of those who really need them. It's no wonder all the good eggs and cuckoo nuts are scrambling and the squirrels and chipmunks are hunkering all their worldly possessions in their faces and the beavers are bunkering just below the surface.

They need to steer clear of the little mosquitoes who buzz through security without their IDs and share their disease with the rats who are racing and chasing their tails. I have no idea how the snail feels strolling along with a snowballs chance of beating the turtle, who coincidentally is competing with Mertl the speedy long-eared hare . . . I mean rabbit . . . dagnabit and I hope this is abundantly clear.

Circling above there's vultures and long-necked geese swarming like flies, invading our skies and dropping all their business on us. And ten thousand too tall, too nosey long-necked giraffes are looking over our

fences and over our shoulders invading our
privacy, all the while blocking our one good
shot at what really matters to us.

There are a million and one electric monkeys
swinging from tree to tree seizing all the
excellent opportunities before they even
have a chance to present themselves to us.

I wonder, "Where do they get the energy?
Stop! Focus and breathe."

Just who is flipping the bill and greasing the
palms of all those penguins disguised as
doctors and lawyers, not really knowing
what they're doing but more than willing to
take a quack at it. It's pretty hard to track
the winners; or determine who's really a
victim of chance or a victim of circumstance.

We have kangaroos carrying babies and
babies carrying even more babies and I can't
see no visible means of support and I only
report this because it seems nobody cares.

There's a need for a break, to contemplate
and consultate with the wise old owl who
just happens to reside in a tall old oak tree

located in an isolated place in an obscure spot that nobody knows. Ah, what could he know anyway? We're down to earth and he's way up there all alone not really zoned into the problems at hand. How could he understand better than my friends who are directly affected by this circumstance?

I need to rest before I continue . . . I go to the fair to take time to forget and I go to a window to order a ticket to a very fast roller coaster and I find it ain't really helping because it's just exposing me to new peaks 'n valleys and I truly need to rally my emotions before the explosion . . .

Stop! Focus and breathe.

Well, the vacation is over 'n it's time to get sober 'n have no remorse. And coping is moving weary bones from microscope to the telescope to get a new view of reality, of course.

Below the thunder and storms I see remoras helping sharks and doctors helping people avoid the gurney to prolong this journey and I wonder why they do it. And I wonder why

are all those chimpanzees continue to groom
their mates? And why do all these little
rabbits continue to mate?

Wait! It's to create more rabbits, of course.

And why do painters paint, and sculptors
continue to grind clay? It's to make
something from nothing, and because they
have something to say and this is the way
they do it.

I seen little boys 'n girls float in on butterfly
wings and innocently do it with lemonade
stands and money making schemes causing
their bank accounts to burst at the seams,
filled with hundreds and hundreds of
pennies and childhood dreams.

It seems unduly extreme to put pressure like
this on our labor force, this being an
exaggeration of course, but when we see or
hear thoughts getting carried away we need
to understand, time waits for no man.

It's a bullet train that moves us from cradle
to tomb and some get off so fast, sooner
rather than later, 'n some seem to ride on it

forever and ever, constantly looking for something better and better and in the end, we're not doomed to this struggle and strife as it seems no matter, life comes 'n goes, and too soon it's past.

And then there are folks who are older than dirt, their time has gone with their friends who left earlier than expected and they can't seem to exit because the train don't stop, it's moving too fast. All they can do is focus and breathe 'cause all the friends they have left are just reflections and collections of faces in books and they just want to talk to relate to anybody but they can't because the phones don't work 'cause the internets down and the gall darn Facebook is just too confusing!

"Stop! Focus and . . .

Stop! Focus . . .

Just stop!"

14. Blues to Silver and Black Again

(6 minutes 16 Seconds)
By T.L. Raasch

The Blues are a recognition of despair and hardship. The songs in this genre are generally very popular and very appealing to the masses.

This song presents a new mood called the "The Silvers". It's a recognition of the things that are good and going right.

Of course there are folks out there who can't buy this newfound upbeat, passionate view of life. I'll bet you can guess the individual who presents and represents a counter argument against "The Silvers".

<u>The Lyrics</u>

(Yeah, Yeah . . . yeah, yeah, yeah, yeah, yeah)
Hmmm . . . It's cool to have "The Blues".
(Ah, yeah, yeah, yeah)
It's even cooler to say "You don't know the blues,
You can't know the blues".
(Yeah, yeah, yeah)
People like to talk about their down-and-outs,

(Yeah, yeah)
And they love to compare their depression bouts.
(Yeah, yeah, yeah)
"Ohhhh, the Blues" It even sounds cool.
I've got the "so-sad-I'm-mad-that-I'm-glad"
(Yeah, yeah)
I ain't no fool, I got the Blues."
(Shoe-be-dop Bah-bah), (Shoe-be-dop Bah-bah)

You almost want to be part of it, them there blues.
(Shoe-be-dop), (Shoe-be-dop)
But why?
They're painful, they're sad.
They're the "things gone wrong" and the "I don't
belong".
Yeah, they make a good song.
(Shoe-be-dop), (Shoe-be-dop), (Shoe-be-dop dap-do)

We don't even have a color that talks about the
other side,
(Shoe-be-dop), (Shoe-be-dop)
'cause people hide from the "what's gone right"
And that "at-the-end-of-the-tunnel light."
(Shoe-be-dop), (Shoe-be-dop)
You know, the "I'm okay, better than okay, things
are great!" state.
And it's definitely not cool, to be the fool of no
complaints.
(Nan-nan-nan-nan-nan no-no-complaints)

A musical transition . . .

Introducing a new mood,
"The Silvers".
The color of the "lining inside-the-cloud"
That hangs over the head of those with the blues.
(Ohhhhhhhh noooooo!)
They're gonna hate this news.
And I got "The Silvers", for just about anything you
choose.
(Ohhh no!)
Yeah my Silvers are so good I'll never become
unglued,
Even when I lose, And let's not misconstrue, I hate
to lose.
(Nan-nan-nan-nan-nan no), (Nan-nan-nan-nan-
nan no)

I got "The Silvers" for the weather.
If you're talkin' rain, I'm talkin' drink, and food for
the brain.
(Nan-nan-nan-nan-nan no I'm not talkin')
You're talkin' wind, I'm talkin' it fills my sails and
lifts my spirit.
You can almost hear it.
(Nan-nan-nan-nan-nan na-na-na . . .)

You're talkin' heat,
I'll say I don't sweat, I perspire and inspire.
"The Silvers" don't let you get tired,
They make you rewire, join the choir
And sing 'round the fire.

"The Blues" are about an empty pocket book,
The broken-hearted, the misunderstood . . .
And when you take a look
"The Silvers" are a motor started on that little
train that could".

An "Eeorye Interruption"

I'm regretful, and I don't mean to be disrespectful
But the Silvers you speak of, they seem rather grey
'n that ol' cloud just brings more 'n more rain, day
after day.

Blackness surrounds me just like a cacklin' crow,
So I don't really see what you say as just so,

All the dampness just makes my ears droop,
'n I lost my pink tail ribbon, now I can't even poop.

Why is my head down?
Around my eyes the flies are a-buzzin'
Why is my head down?
I can't think of a reason, it's more like a dozen.

Please remember the new mood
The Silvers
The color of the lining inside the cloud that hangs
over your head
Remember what I said
You can almost hear it
You can't break my spirit . . .

15. Forever Young

(2 minutes 45 Seconds)
Written by Bob Dylan

The last song is another Bob Dylan song; It's a simple "Best wishes" type song that ends my "concert". Please don't fight the urge to sing along.

<u>The Lyrics</u>

(Last one, good night everybody)
(And stay forever young)
May God bless and keep you always
May your wishes all come true
May you always do for others
And let others do for you
May you build a ladder to the stars
And climb on every rung
May you stay forever young

(Sweet . . . nicely done!)
May you grow up to be righteous
(I can't help it, I got to join in)
May you grow up to be true
May you always know the truth
And see the lights surrounding you
May you always be courageous
Stand upright and be strong
May you stay forever young

(Okay, big finish!)
May your hands always be busy
May your feet always be swift
May you have a strong foundation
When the winds of changes shift
May your heart always be joyful
And may your song always be sung
And may you stay forever young

(Jackie Jesson the Sax)
(And Tommy Thomas on the guitar)

www.ingramcontent.com/pod-product-compliance
Lightning Source LLC
Chambersburg PA
CBHW070727260726
48660CB00007B/2763